COUNT DRACULATIONS!

COUNT DRACULATIONS!

MONSTER RIDDLES

compiled by Charles Keller

illustrated by Edward Frascino

Prentice-Hall Books for Young Readers
A Division of Simon & Schuster, Inc.
New York

Published by Prentice-Hall Books for Young Readers
A Division of Simon & Schuster, Inc.
Simon & Schuster Building
Rockefeller Center
1230 Avenue of the Americas
New York, NY 10020

10 9 8 7 6 5 4 3

Prentice-Hall Books for Young Readers
is a trademark of Simon & Schuster, Inc.

Manufactured in the United States of America

Library of Congress Cataloging in Publication Data
Keller, Charles
   Count Draculations!
   1. Riddles, Juvenile.   2. Monsters—Juvenile humor.
I. Frascino, Edward.   II. Title.
PN6371.5.K384   1986   818'.5402   85-25778
ISBN 0-13-183641-2

To Nicole and Leigh

What do you say to a new vampire?
"Count Draculations!"

What is wolfman's favorite hotel?
The Howliday Inn.

Where does a ghost park his car?
In a mirage.

Why do witches get A's in school?
Because they are good at spelling.

What do ghosts chew?
Boo-ble gum.

What is big, hairy, and flies 1,500 miles per hour?
King Kongcorde.

What do ghosts eat for dinner?
Spook-ghetti.

How do you get into a locked cemetery?
With a skeleton key.

What kind of phone calls do ghosts make?
Ghost to ghost.

Who did the vampire invite to his family reunion?
All his blood relatives.

What kind of milk does the invisible man drink?
Evaporated.

What does a werewolf eat for a snack?
Ladyfingers.

Why did Frankenstein's monster go to the psychiatrist?
He thought he had a screw loose.

Why did King Kong join the marines?
He wanted to learn about gorilla warfare.

What is a monster's favorite food?
Ghoulash.

Why did the invisible man go crazy?
Out of sight, out of mind.

What do you call a werewolf in sheep's clothing?
A were-wool-f.

What is a monster's favorite drink?
Ghoul-aid.

What do you call a monster's sweetheart?
His ghoul-friend.

What do you call a skeleton that won't get out of bed?
Lazy bones.

Why did the monster's mother knit him three socks?
She heard he grew another foot.

What do you call a vampire's dog?
A blood hound.

What is it called when demons show off?
A demon-stration.

Why do people always take advantage of Dracula?
They never give a sucker an even break.

How does a witch tell time?
With a witch watch.

What kind of jewels do ghosts like?
Tombstones.

Where does a vampire take a bath?
In a bat tub.

What are monster sidewalks made of?
Concreep.

How can you tell if a vampire has been in your tomato juice?
By the two tiny teeth marks on the can.

What happened when Dracula auditioned for a movie role?
He got a bit part.

When does a monster give his mother a gift?
On Mummy's Day.

Why did King Kong climb to the top of the tall building?
Because he couldn't fit into the elevator.

What will chase a vampire away?
A ring around the collar.

What flowers do ghosts grow?
Mari-ghouls and morning gories.

Why do they put fences around cemeteries?
Because people are dying to get in.

What do you get when you cross a vampire and a hyena?
A monster that laughs at the sight of blood.

What kind of blood does Dracula have?
Donated.

How do you keep a ghost from trespassing on your farm?
Put up "No Haunting" signs.

Why does a vampire brush his teeth?
To prevent bat breath.

Why can't you tell when a ghost is sitting in your chair?
Because the ghost is clear.

How do you make a witch scratch?
Take away her W.

What is the mother or father of an invisible baby called?
A trans-parent.

What should you do if you meet King Kong?
Give him a large banana.

Why is Dracula a great artist?
He can draw blood.

What does a vampire put on before he goes to the beach?
Moontan lotion.

What did the boy vampire say to the girl vampire?
"I like your blood type."

How do you spot a vampire jockey?
He always wins by a neck.

Why aren't vampires good gamblers?
They always make sucker bets.

Why does a skeleton go to the library?
To bone up on a few things.

What kind of horse does the headless horseman ride?
A nightmare.

What happened when the vampire started writing poetry?
Things went from bat to verse.

What does a vampire say to his girlfriend?
"Let's neck."

Why are ghosts lonely all the time?
Because they haven't got any body.

What law keeps monsters on the ground?
The law of grave-ity.

Why did Dracula go to the dentist?
To improve his bite.

What's the best way to get rid of a demon?
Exorcise a lot.

What kind of car does a ghost drive?
A Boo-ick.

What position does a monster play on a hockey team?
Ghoulie.

Where do baby monsters come from?
Frankenstorks.

How did they finally catch Count Dracula?
He tried to rob the blood bank.

Where do famous dragons go?
To the Hall of Flame.

What's green and lives in the Himalayas?
The Abominable Snow Pickle.

Where do ghosts hang out when they are not haunting?
On the clothesline.

What do vampires hate to have for dinner?
A steak. It gives them heartburn.

What animal do vampires like best?
A giraffe.

What did the vampire say to the dentist?
"Fangs very much."

What happens when you don't pay an exorcist?
You get repossessed.

What does the Abominable Snowman have for lunch?
Cold cuts.

What do you get when you cross a werewolf with a hair stylist?
A monster with curly hair all over its body.

How do mummies behave?
In a grave manner.

What was Dr. Jekyll's favorite game?
Hyde and seek.

Why did the little ghost measure himself against the wall?
He wanted to see if he gruesome.

When do ghosts have to stop scaring people?
When they lose their haunting license.

What does Dracula's wife put in his room when he has a cold?
A Vamporizer.

Why are ghosts very simple things?
They can be easily seen through.

Why did the vampire join the navy?
He wanted to sail on the bat-tleship.

Who won the monster beauty contest?
Nobody.

What kind of car does the wolfman drive?
A Wolfswagen.

What holiday does Dracula celebrate in November?
Fangsgiving.

What is a stupid monster?
A dummy mummy.

Why are vampires crazy?
They are often bats.

What happens when you have a fight with Dracula?
He really chews you out.

Where is the best place for a vampire to take a vacation?
The South Pole. No sunrise to worry about for six months.

What's green and only comes out at night?
Vampickle.

Where does a monster's wife have her hair done?
At the ugly parlor.

What monster flies his kite in a rain storm?
Benjamin Frankenstein.

Why did the ghost attend the banquet?
He was the after-dinner spooker.

What do ghosts serve for dessert?
Ice scream and devil dogs.

What do ghosts say before starting a meeting?
"Ladies and gentlemen, please be sheeted."

What's a monster's favorite play?
Romeo and Ghouliet.

What does a modern witch fly?
An electric broom.

Why did they send the mummy in as a pinch hitter?
The game was all wrapped up.

Why did Cyclops have to close his school?
He only had one pupil.

Where do ghosts get their mail?
At the dead letter office.

What do witches put on their hair?
Scare spray.

What do you call a witch's motorcycle?
A baa-rr-oom stick.

How does a vampire make a living?
He moonlights.

What present does a rich vampire give his son?
A red sports coffin.

What did the vampire say when he called the funeral parlor?
"Do you deliver?"

What do you call two monsters?
A gruesome twosome.

What did one ghost say to the other ghost?
"Do you believe in people?"

What expression does a zombie have on his face?
Deadpan.

What do you get when you cross Bambi and a ghost?
Bamboo.

What does a vampire say when he is asked to dinner?
"No fangs, I just ate necks door."

What kind of crew does a ghost ship have?
A skeleton crew.

What did the vampire want for Christmas?
His two front teeth.

How can you tell a boy mummy from a girl mummy?
One is wrapped in blue and the other in pink.

What do ghosts call their navy?
The Ghost Guard.

Why don't vampires start baseball games in the afternoon?
Because their bats don't come out until nighttime.

Where do ghosts go when they get sick?
To the witch doctor.

Who would win a race between two vampires?
They would finish neck and neck.

What is a blood count?
Count Dracula.

How do you make a skeleton sad?
Take away his funny bone.

How does a two-headed monster speak?
In double talk.

What kind of music do ghosts like to hear?
Haunting refrains.

Why does a skeleton drink a lot of milk?
It's good for the bones.

What does a ghost soldier say when he hears a strange noise?
"Halt! Who ghosts there?"

What do you call art objects made by a witch?
Witchcraft.

Why did the ghost go to the doctor?
He needed a boo-ster shot.

What's a haunted chicken?
A poultry-geist.

What's a nice present for a baby ghost?
A pair of boo-ties.

What did the 2,000-year-old boy say when they dug him up?
"I want my mummy."

What's a monster's favorite baseball game?
A doubleheader.

What's the favorite game of vampires?
Bat-minton.

Why do vampires like people who get hot under the collar?
They occasionally enjoy a hot meal.

What is a haunted wigwam?
A creepy teepee.

What is a gravedigger's favorite dance?
The vaults.

Why was the skeleton a coward?
Because he had no guts.

Why do ghosts like to ride in elevators?
It raises their spirits.

What room doesn't a ghost go in?
The living room.

What is Dracula's favorite movie?
"The Vampire Strikes Back."

What does Dracula take when he has a cold?
Coffin medicine.

How do you make a strawberry shake?
Take it to a horror movie.

How did King Kong like his steak?
Medium roar.

What do witches want in a hotel?
Broom service.

What weighs five tons and eats tin cans?
Goatzilla.

What's a chicken's favorite horror movie?
The Eggs-orcist.

Why do witches fly on broomsticks?
It beats walking.

Why did Frankenstein's monster win the election?
Because he got all the volts.

Why was the mummy late for dinner?
He was all wrapped up in his work.

Why was there no food left at the monster party?
Because everyone was a goblin.

What kind of pants do ghosts wear?
Boo-jeans.

Where do witches learn to cast spells?
In charm school.

What skeleton ruled France?
Napoleon Bone-apart.

What's a ghost's favorite dessert?
Booberry pie.

What do you call a witch's suitcase?
A hag bag.

What do you get when you cross a vampire with a dwarf?
A monster that sucks blood out of your knees.

How do ghosts like their eggs?
Terri-fried.

When do ghosts haunt skyscrapers?
When they are in high spirits.

Where does a witch keep her spaceship?
In the broom closet.

How wide is a cemetery?
A grave yard.